Scroll Saw

Christmas Ornaments

by Tom Zieg

FOX BOOKS
Fox Chapel Publishing Co Inc.

D0507560

Publisher: Alan Giagnocavo
Project Editor: Ayleen Stellhorn
Desktop Specialist: Linda L. Eberly, Eberly Designs Inc.
Cover Photography: Carl Shuman, Owl Hill Studios

ISBN # 1-56523-123-6

To order your copy of this book,
please send check or money order
for $9.95 plus $2.50 shipping to:
Fox Books
1970 Broad Street
East Petersburg, PA 17520

Manufactured in the United States

Dedication

To Judy, Andrea and Rebecca

Acknowledgements

I would like to thank the Lord for giving me the ability and opportunity to do what I enjoy. I would also like to thank my family, neighbors and friends for so graciously accepting the Christmas ornaments and decorations I have given them through the years and for providing me with the encouragement to keep going.

A special thank you is due Mike Hoag for providing the woodcarved ornaments used in this book.

TABLE OF CONTENTS

Introduction

Christmas is perhaps the season of the year most associated with decoration. Many of the decorations are used only for Christmas and are carefully stored away during the rest of the year. Although new items appear each year, it is those old favorites that remind us of Christmases past. Some of those decorations are rooted deeply in tradition.

The Christmas tree, with its bright lights, ornaments and draped garlands and tinsel, has its place in all the festive decorations. No matter what size the tree is, it commands the attention of those who see it and often remains the center of the home's holiday celebration.

No one is quite certain just when the Christmas tree became part of the Christmas tradition. The earliest historical references place it in the 1500s. Although primitive cultures used evergreens as a symbol of eternal life, trimmed greenery with decorations and brought nature indoors, the oldest pieces of documentation associate the "Christmas tree" with Latvia and Estonia.

Because of the association of the tree with pagan religions, the use of the tree was discouraged by the Roman Catholic church. But the tradition had become so ingrained in German culture that its use was eventually accepted and it was even transformed into a Christian symbol.

The Germans are credited with the tradition of taking the tree into the home and decorating it for the holidays. Their early Christmas trees were placed on tables and decorated with dolls, paper roses, apples, wafers, gold foil, sweets and wax tapers. During the early 1800s, glass blowers in Lauscha, Germany, began making glass bubbles (kugels) and decided the small ones looked nice on the Christmas tree. The song "O Tannenbaum! O Tannenbaum! (O Christmas Tree! O Christmas Tree!)" reflects the love the Germans had for the evergreen tree.

After the custom of decorating the tree had spread through Germany, it reached Finland, Denmark, Sweden, Norway, Austria and France. Although the Christmas tree did not begin appearing in England until 1822, the first record of Christmas trees in use in America was in Bethlehem, Pennsylvania, as early as 1747. However, it is believed these were not real evergreens, but wooden pyramids covered with evergreen boughs. Not until 1819 or 1820 was the second use of Christmas trees in America recorded. This record was in the form of two sketchbook drawings by a Philadelphia artist named John Lewis Krimmel.

Around 1900, only one in five American families had a Christmas tree in their home. By 1910, most families in many parts of the country practiced the custom. The Christmas tree did not appear in the southern and western parts of the United States until 1915. Since 1930, the American Christmas tradition has not been complete without a Christmas tree.

Although commercially produced ornaments reached America around 1860 as possessions of German immigrants, American Christmas trees were trimmed with simple decorations. Because store-bought ornaments were not readily available, people used cookies, candy, fruit, colored paper ornaments, tufts of cotton, gilded nuts and nutshells and strings of popcorn and cranberries. The Americans developed the floor-to-ceiling Christmas tree, decorated with dolls, honey and ginger cakes cut into animal shapes, stuffed animals, fruit and nut-filled hanging baskets and cornucopias, small toys, chessmen, puzzles, photographs and even moss.

Commercially produced Christmas ornaments that could be kept from year to year began to arrive in America from Germany in the 1870s. The first were cast from soft tin alloy by Nuremberg tinsmiths and were followed by molded wax ornaments from German toymakers.

Around the turn of the century, American Christmas trees had few store-bought ornaments and were still decorated in part with edibles. Women's magazines from the 1890s featured articles on do-it-yourself homemade ornaments. Homemade ornaments had become a "fashionable rage."

As more and more commercially produced ornaments arrived in America, the homemade decorations began to be replaced. Even the custom of placing gifts on the tree was lost. Small wood toys from German wood carvers and molded glass ornaments from German glass blowers became very popular.

After the outbreak of World War I, German ornaments became difficult to obtain. American companies attempted to manufacture the ornaments, but could not compete with the German quality and price. Germany regained the market in the early 1920s. Glass blowers in Vienna, Poland, Czechoslovakia and Japan began to copy the German ornaments. Yet, from 1930 until the start of World War II, 95 percent of the glass ornaments on American trees were produced in Lauscha, Germany.

As World War II started, a possible embargo of German products to America motivated American companies to begin making the glass ornaments—this time successfully. During the 1950s, the early, simple homemade ornaments for Christmas trees became a thing of the past. American Christmas trees became overloaded with factory-made ornaments, and the making of those ornaments became an important industry of the United States. Between 1950 and the early 1960s, only about 20 percent of America's ornaments came from Germany.

Once again, homemade ornaments are becoming popular. The warmth and sentiment offered in wood ornaments far outweigh that found in glass and plastic store-bought ornaments. As a scroller, you have the opportunity to create beautifully crafted Christmas ornaments that could possibly become tomorrow's antiques. Although I recommend that the ornaments in this book be made from 1/8" Baltic or Russian birch to maintain strength, they can also be made from other materials, such as paper, plastic, brass, copper and aluminum. The ornaments can also be carved into thicker pieces of wood for a completely different look. No matter what materials are used, rest assured that the ornaments made and given to others will be something that can always be treasured.

Cutting out the Ornaments

The patterns in this book are a grouping of religious, traditional, word and fun patterns. They are full size and range from easy (for the scroll saw novice) to some that are quite intricate and require skill and a steady hand. Many will require a 2/0 blade in order to cut the fine detail.

Because of the fine detail, the best material for use is 1/8" Baltic or Russian birch plywood. The plywood provides the strength needed to prevent pieces from breaking off. The orna-ments can be finished clear, painted or stained. The ornaments can also be cut from a thin sheet of aluminum, brass or copper to create a completely different look. Plastic, 1/8" thick, also makes unusual ornaments.

An interesting idea is to stack cut the ornaments from paper. Include a paper ornament in each of the Christmas cards you give. They make an inexpensive gift to give to friends and relatives and are guaranteed to generate compliments on your scrolling ability.

Religious Patterns

Nativity

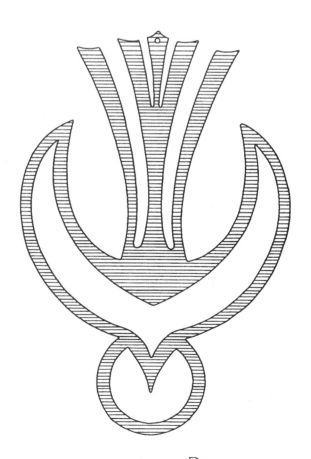

Dove

Angels

Angels

Angels

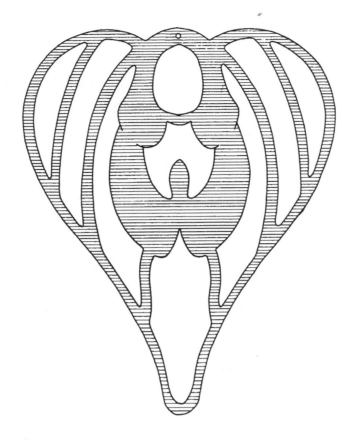

Angels

Following The Star

The Journey

Chi Rho

Cross

Peace

Oil Lamp

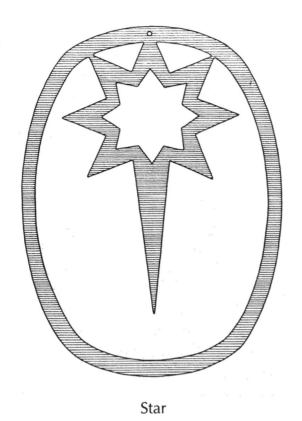

Star

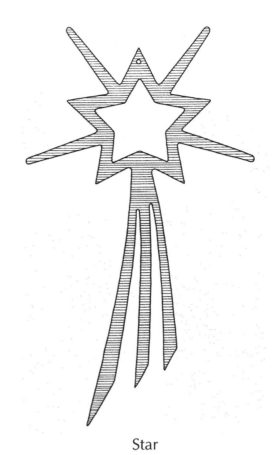

Star

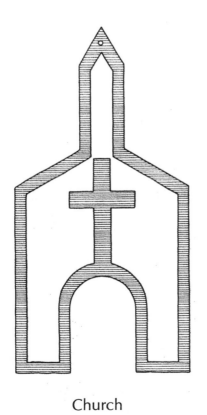

Church

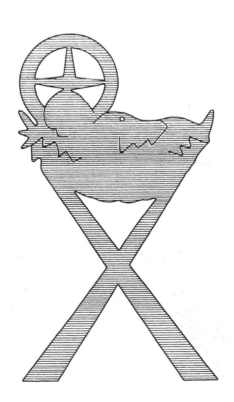

Manger

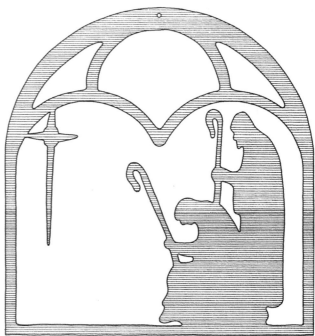

O Holy Night

Nativity

Madonna with Child

Menorah

Church

Crown

Dove

O Holy Night

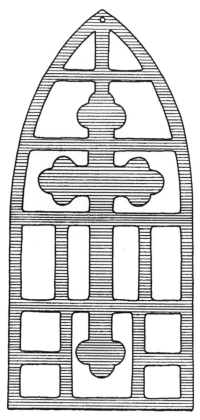

Cross in Window

Star

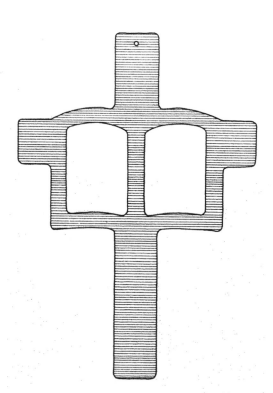

Cross with Bible

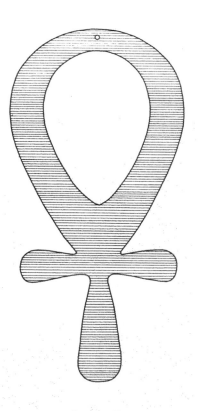

Ankh Cross

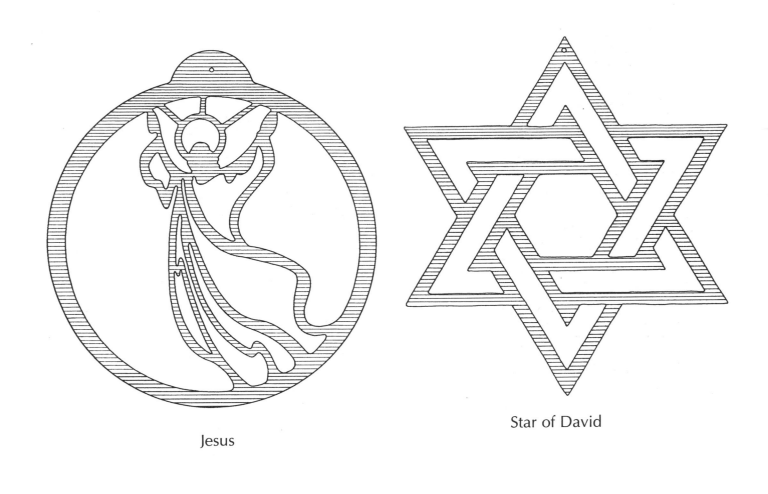

Jesus

Star of David

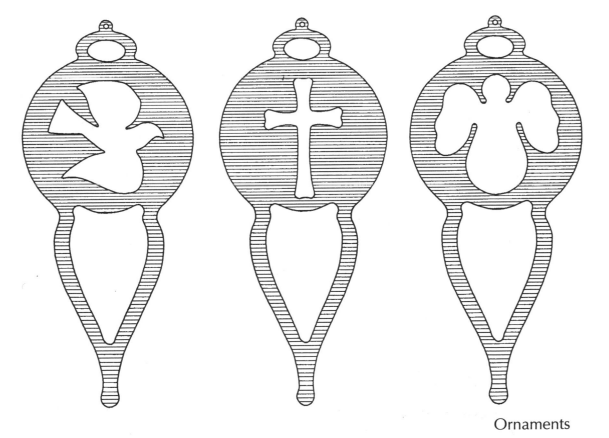

Ornaments

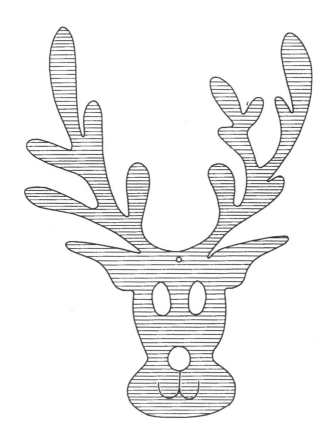

Reindeer

Snowman

Locomotive

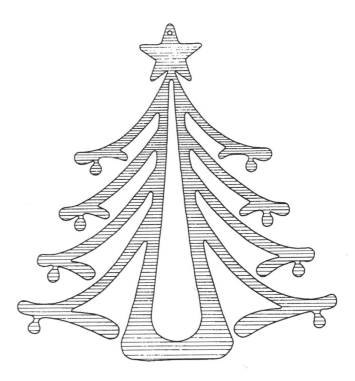

Christmas Tree

Locomotive

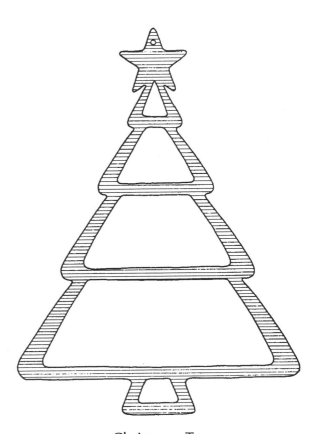

Christmas Tree

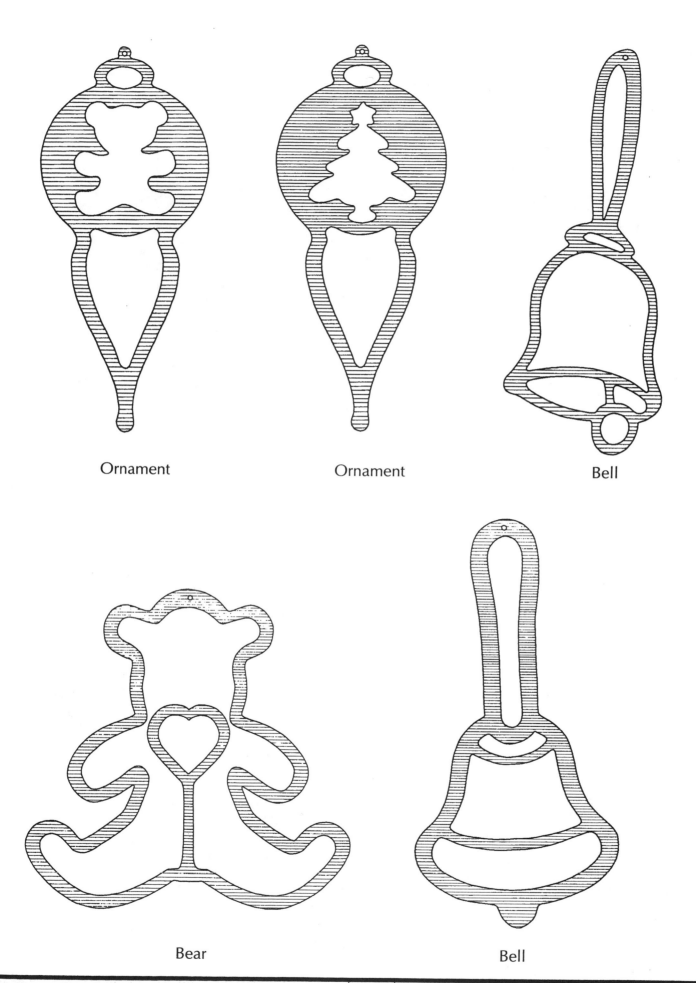

Ornament

Ornament

Bell

Bear

Bell

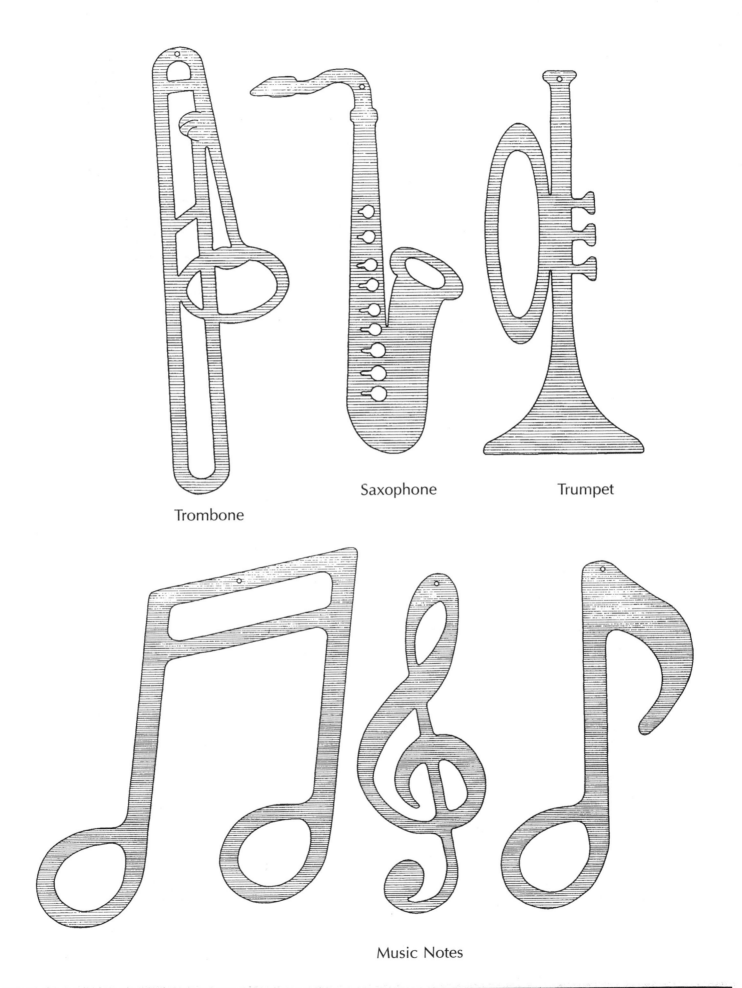

Saxophone

Trumpet

Trombone

Music Notes

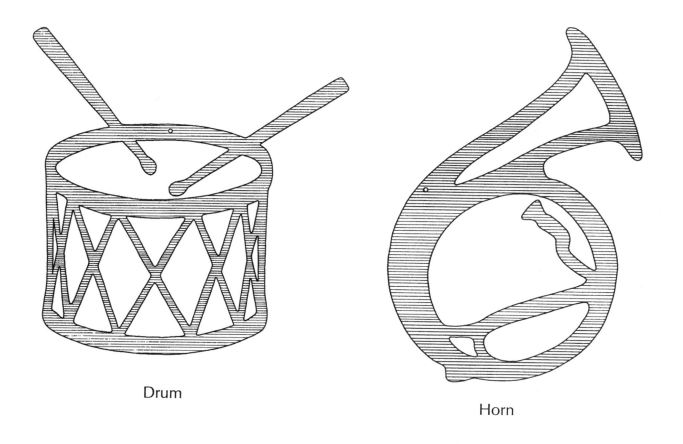

Drum

Horn

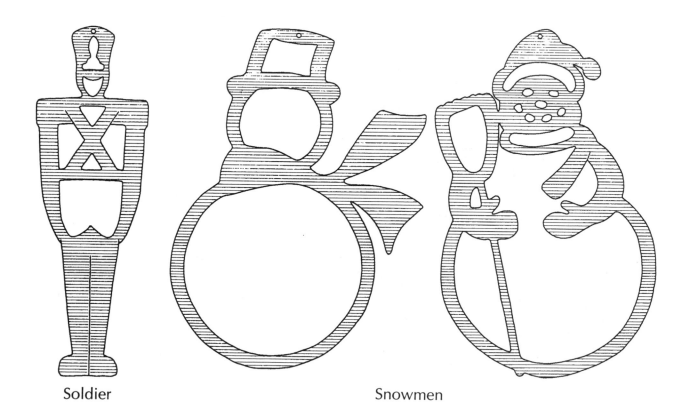

Soldier

Snowmen

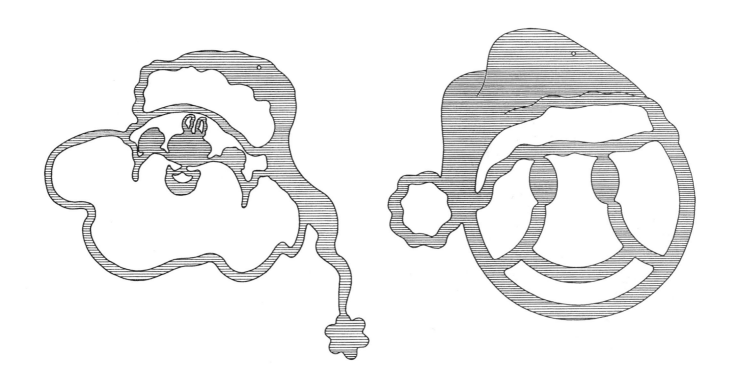

Santa Faces

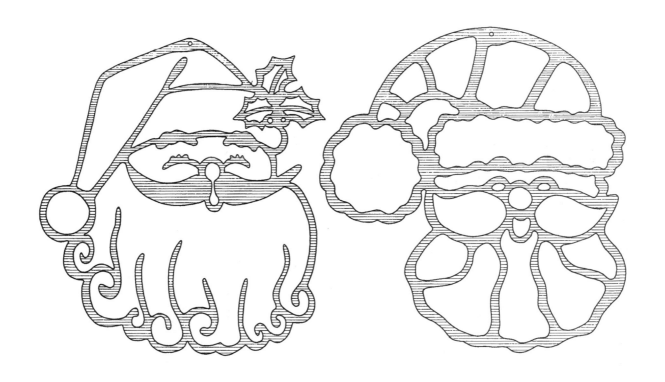

Santa Faces

Bells

Bell with Carolers

Horn

Bell

Candle

Poinsettia

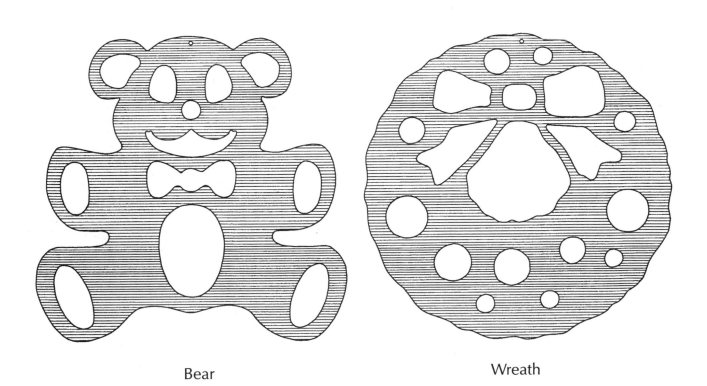

Bear

Wreath

Sleigh

Christmas Tree with Dove

Stocking

Santa Face

Christmas Tree

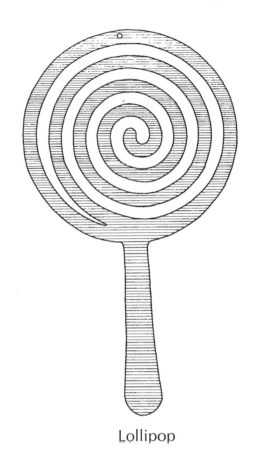

Lollipop

House

Lantern

Snowflake

Candy Cane Heart

Candy Cane

Christmas Present

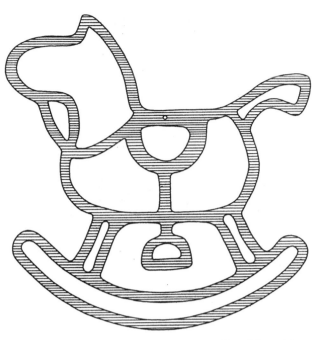

Rocking Horse

Holly

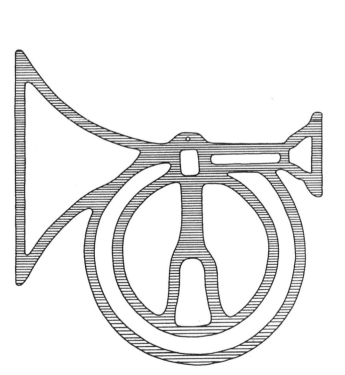

Horn

Holly

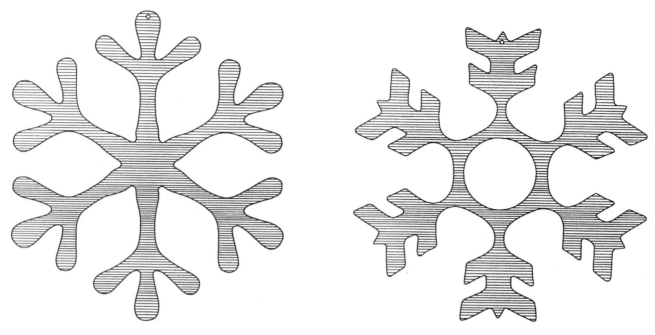

Snowflakes

Rocking Horse

Ice Skate

Snowflake

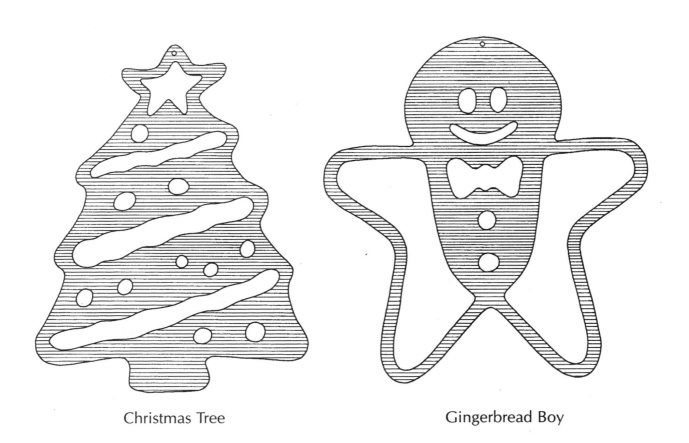

Christmas Tree   Gingerbread Boy

Ornaments

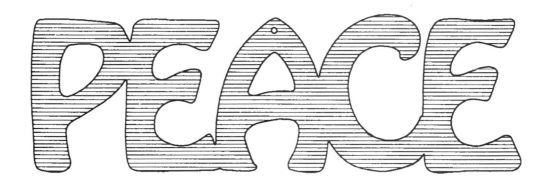

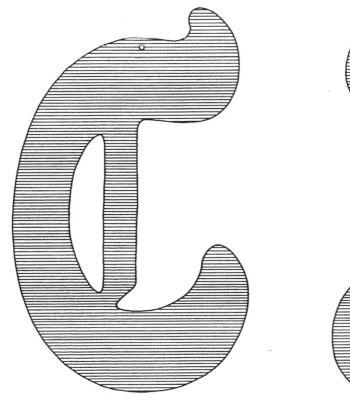
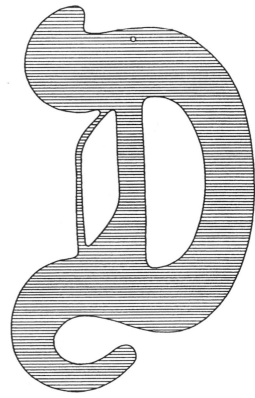

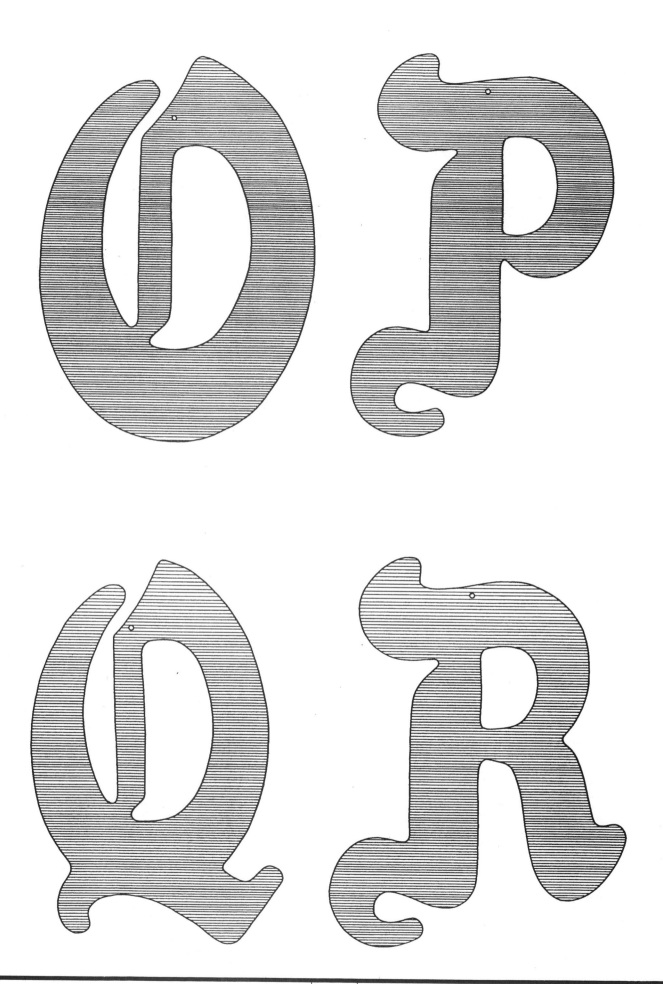

Ornaments

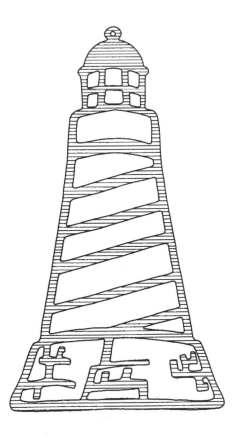

Lighthouse

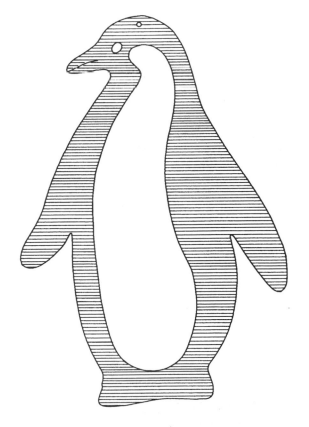

Penguin

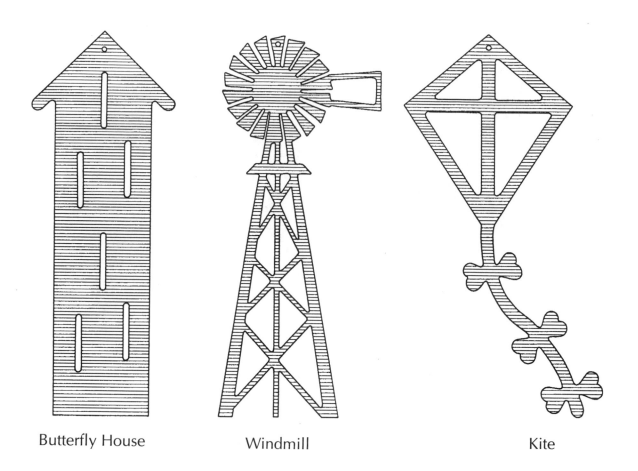

Butterfly House   Windmill   Kite

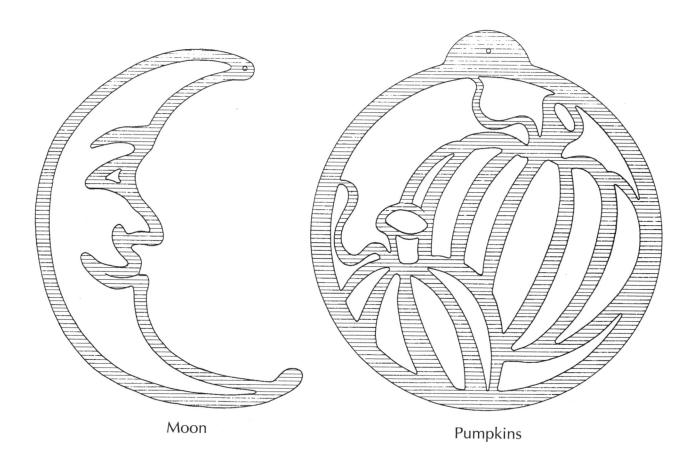

Moon   Pumpkins

Palm Trees

Frog

Bicycle

Mushroom

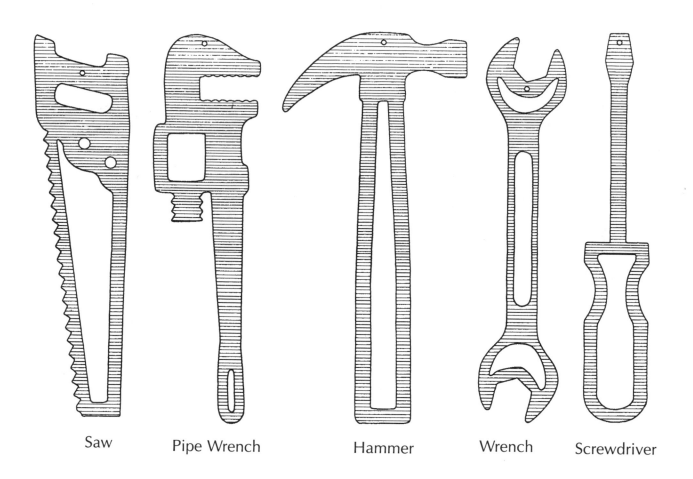

Saw   Pipe Wrench   Hammer   Wrench   Screwdriver

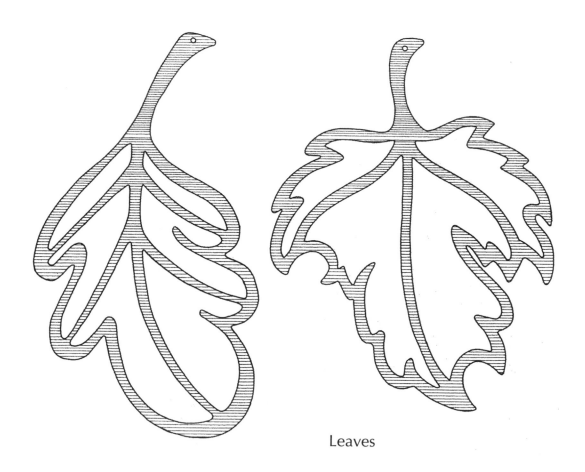

Leaves

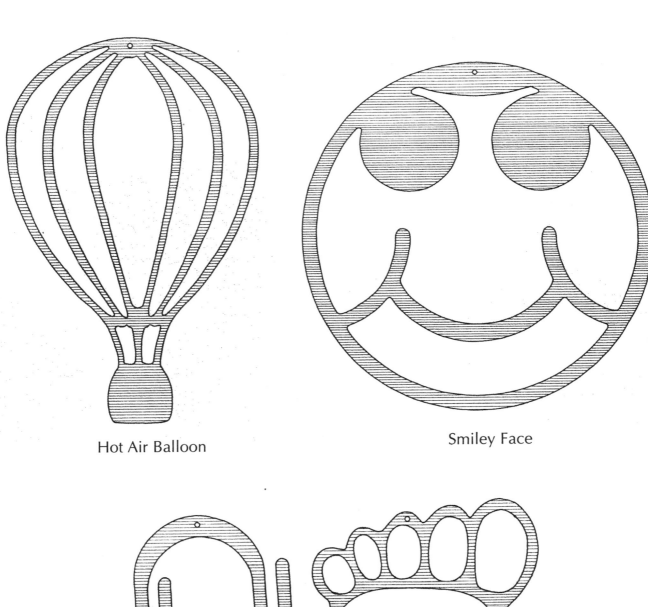

Hot Air Balloon

Smiley Face

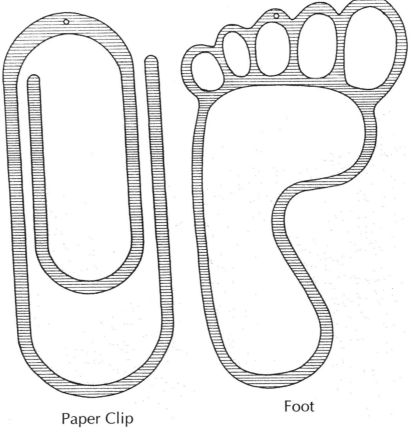

Paper Clip

Foot

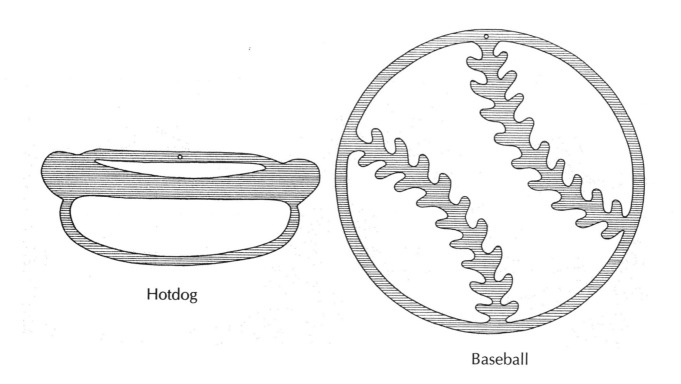

Hotdog

Baseball

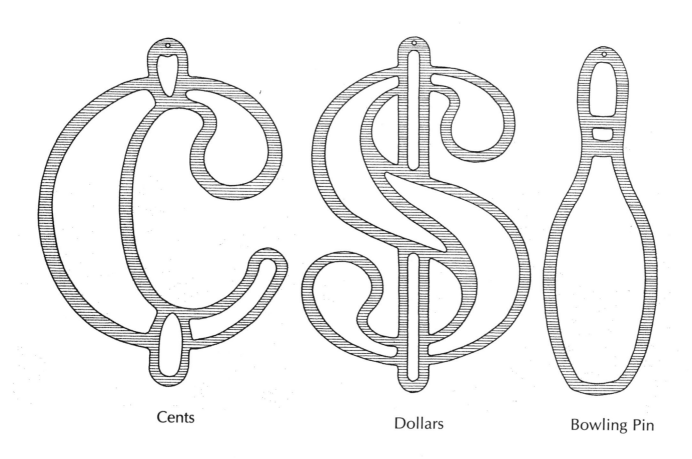

Cents

Dollars

Bowling Pin

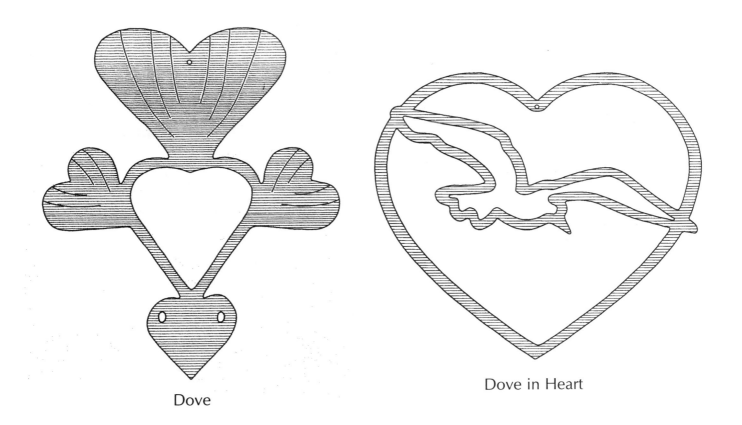

Dove

Dove in Heart

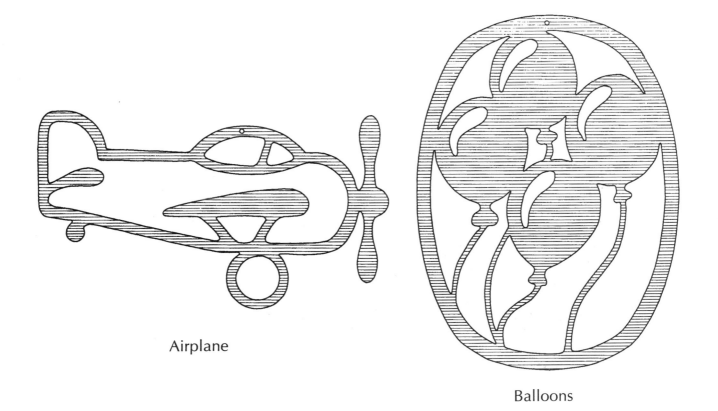

Airplane

Balloons

Butterflies

Butterflies

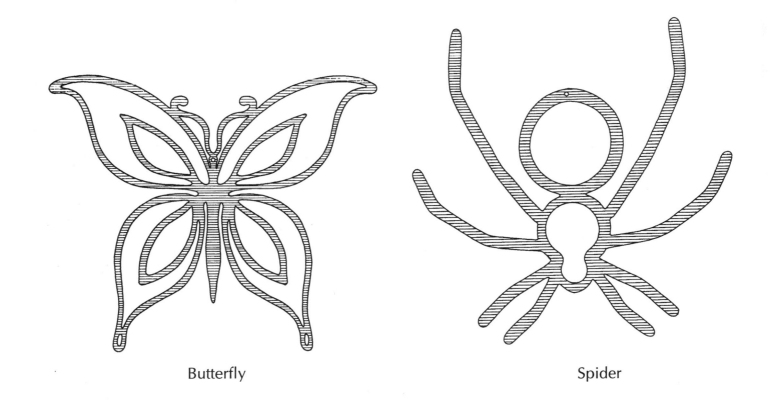

Butterfly

Spider

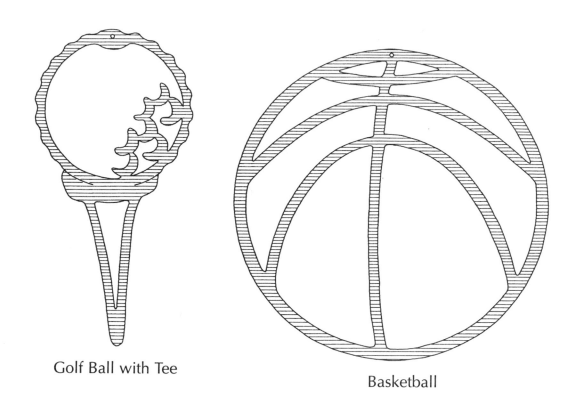

Golf Ball with Tee

Basketball

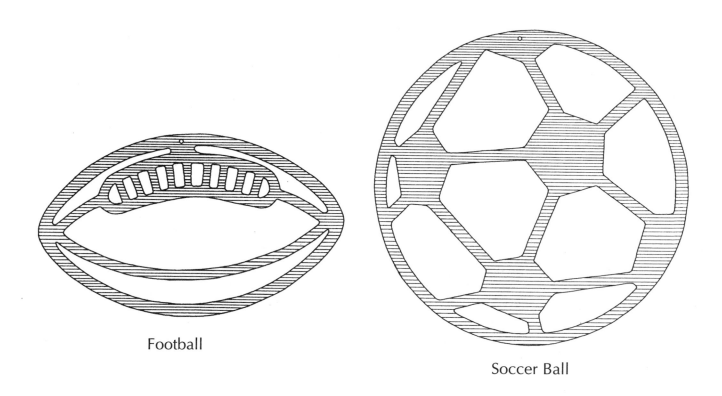

Football

Soccer Ball

Volleyball

Sunrise

Hearts

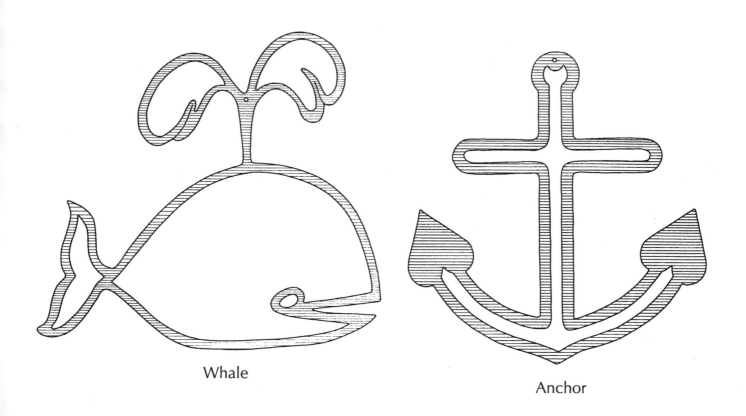

Whale

Anchor

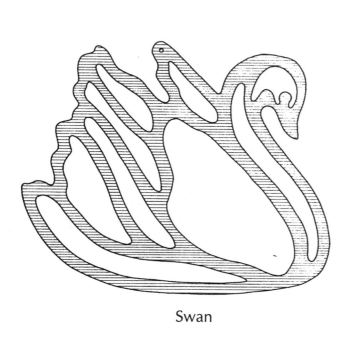

Swan

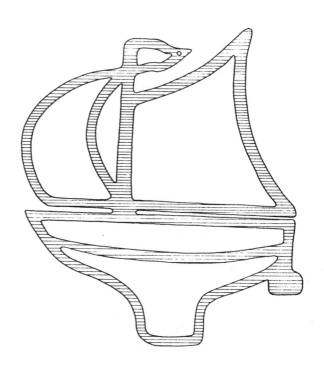

Sailboat

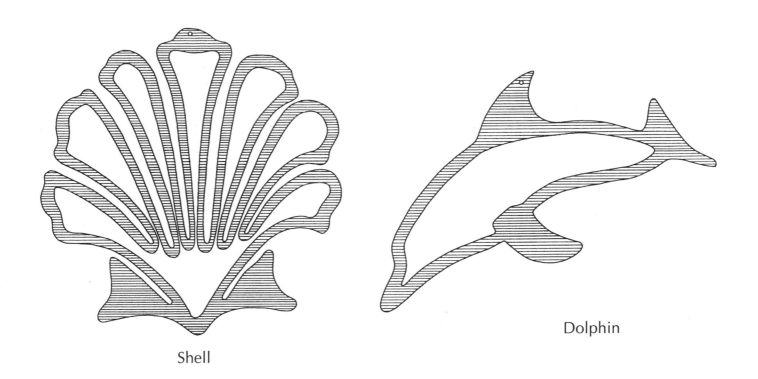

Shell

Dolphin

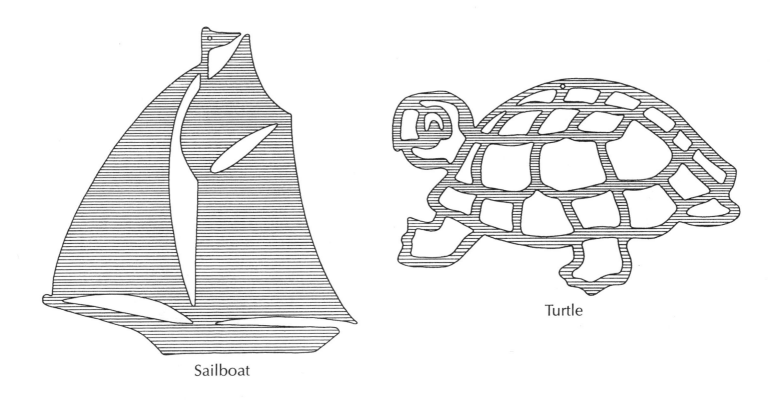

Sailboat

Turtle

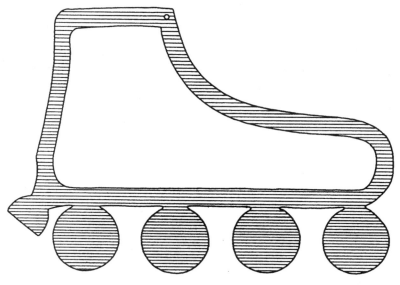

In-Line Skate

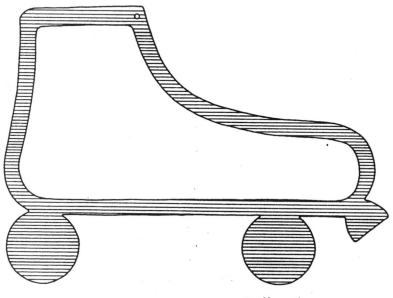

Roller Skate

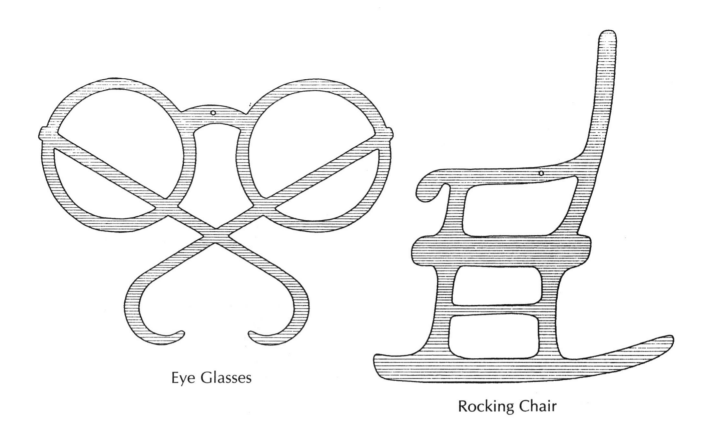

Eye Glasses

Rocking Chair

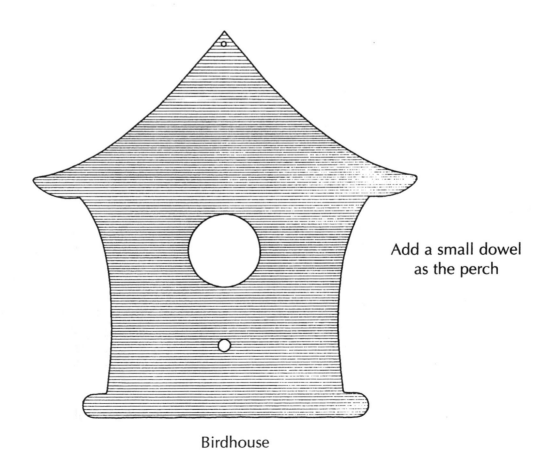

Add a small dowel
as the perch

Birdhouse

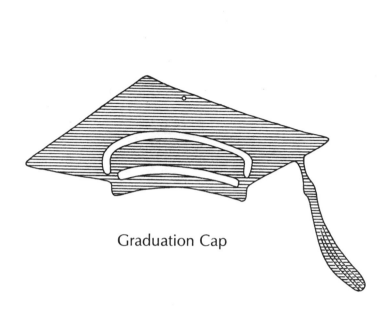

Graduation Cap

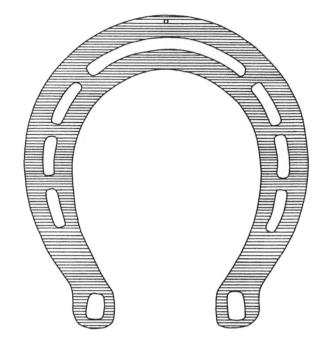

Horseshoe

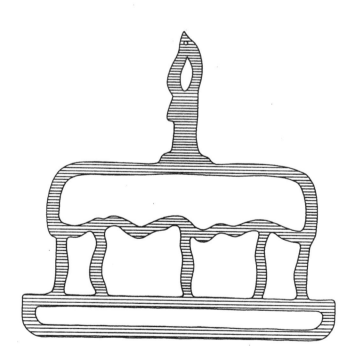

Birthday Cake

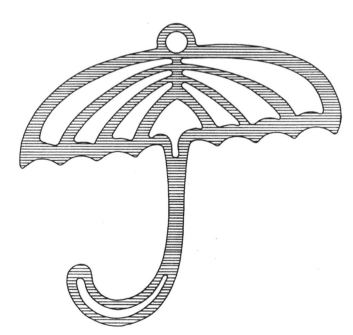

Umbrella

Snail

Noel

Cat

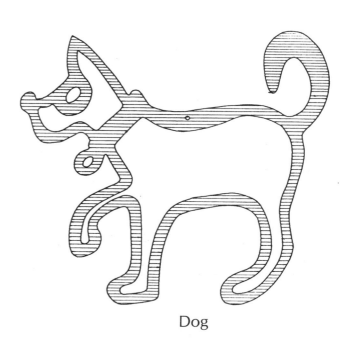

Dog